Dear Pilg

JOHN F. DEANE was born on Achill ... He founded Poetry Ireland – the National Poetry Socie ...nd *The Poetry Ireland Review* in 1978, and is the founder of The Dedalus Press, of which he was editor from 1985 until 2006. In 2008 he was visiting scholar in the Burns Library of Boston College. He was Teilhard de Chardin Fellow in Christian Studies at Loyola University, Chicago, in 2016 and taught a course in poetry. John F. Deane's poetry has been translated and published in France, Bulgaria, Macedonia, Romania, Italy, Slovakia, Sweden and other countries. His poems in Italian won the 2002 Premio Internazionale di Poesia Città di Marineo. His fiction has been published by Blackstaff Press in Belfast; his most recent novel *Where No Storms Come* was published by Blackstaff in 2011. He is the recipient of the O'Shaughnessy Award for Irish Poetry and the Marten Toonder Award for Literature. John F. Deane is a member of Aosdána, the body established by the Arts Council to honour artists 'whose work had made an outstanding contribution to the arts in Ireland.' His poetry has been shortlisted for the Irish Times Poetry Now Award and the T.S. Eliot Prize. In 1996 Deane was elected Secretary-General of the European Academy of Poetry. In 2007 he was made Chevalier en l'ordre des arts et des lettres by the French government.

JOHN F. DEANE

Dear Pilgrims

CARCANET

First published in Great Britain in 2018 by
Carcanet Press Ltd
Alliance House, 30 Cross Street
Manchester M2 7AQ
www.carcanet.co.uk

A CIP catalogue record for this book is available from the British Library.
ISBN 978 1 784105 86 0

The publisher acknowledges financial assistance from Arts Council England.

Typeset in England by XL Publishing Services, Exmouth

for Thomas Leonard, and for his parents
Mary and Nicholas
and i.m. Peter Leonard

Crocus: A Brief History

The crocus opens out to something
more than crocus, becomes a brief history
of time, the ology of cosmos, as a poem is –

impacted yellow of gold-dust, shape
of a baby-thumb all-tentative, prelude to a new year;
breath of fire from the dark earth, from the closed heart;

the rose-coloured: flush of love,
signature of the overture: – these sudden, these small
preliminaries – polyphony of crocus – demi-semi-quavers

of what will be an oratorio
of hollyhock, lupin, sunflower,
under the gold-full baton of the light.

for Thomas Leonard

Contents

A New Testament

According to Lydia

Violin Concerto

The World is Charged

Pearl

Not Titled

Reynolds, staunch Sagittarian,
aimed always high, both barrels of his shotgun
screwed to the dark shape
in the topmost branches of the dawdling sycamore;
and he, Mister H, was truthful when he said
that he was steeped, steeped, steeped

in luck, though I'd say graced
with sequoia-growth of talent. One shoe
dangling
brought Reynolds to a halt :

yet it is again dark-green wreathe-time
in our world, threaded holly branches with their blood-berries,
pine-cones,
that nature's baby Reynolds knitted fast
with his knuckled fingers and thumbs
out of an overburdening love.

An Elegy

Flora in the roadside ditch
are boasting the water-colour purple of a pride of bishops –
vetch, knapweed, clover and the rosebay willow herb;
and I would make a poem

the way old Bruckner caught a flight of pelicans in his
Ecce sacerdos magnus...
for eight-part choir, key magenta, though these times the spirit
slumps, mal tended in this limping country. Now

a blackcap, fast and furtive, comes to feast on the white berries
of the dogwood hedge; bullfinch,
secretive, subdued, flit in a shock of rose-petal black and white
across the alder thicket

and I am urged to praise, willing to have the poem
speak the improbable wonderful. Today
the poet Seamus Heaney said he was leaving us for a while,
visiting high mountain pastures,

and seeing things.
I have been walking, grieved, the Slievemore heathlands
and watching a sheep-dog,
low-crouched, eager, waiting for the sheepman's whistle;

furze blazed with a cool gold flame; the sheep
were marked with blobs of red and purple dye, cumbered
with dried-in mud; while out on the bay
the Crested Grebe moved, masterful, in brown Connemara tweed.

Epithalamium

for Mary and Nicholas

I see you, stilled, attentive, in arrivals hall, love, yet tentative,
somewhere in the air;
I wished, back then, when the white beauty of the frosted earth
was powering the crocus, hyacinth, and daffodil,

that the most perfect snowflakes fall like kisses on your cheeks;
I prayed that –
to the questions you would need to ask – the answers might always be
the loveliness and wonder

of creation. Hold, then, to astonishment, to the ongoing mystery
of one another, the burgeoning familiar;
we have come to understand that when the singing ends
the song continues,

when the poem is written at last, the poetry begins, we have learned
that patience is difficult at the threshold
and in the forecourt of the heart. Be aware of the possibility of grief
and of the conceivable presence of the angel.

I see you, stilled, attentive, at the altar steps,
the bright loveliness of beginnings like a veil about you,
the hearts and prayers of a community
behind you, and this we pray to the God of sacrament :

that she may grace you both to be
magnificent together, magnificent to one another, magnificent
through the bountiful flight ahead.
We wish you music, the slow, classical dance

of what is past and yet to come, the heady beat
of the fleeting present; we wish you sunlight, the reach and sounding
of the waters about Keem Bay,
the gentle breathing of the Atlantic; that all weathers be a force about
you,

keeping you faithful to the fluency of symphony.
I see you, stilled, attentive, in the bright dawn, love urging the grace
of a sure journey upon you, your destination
a better world, of love and mercy, of justice, happiness and peace.

FIRST TESTAMENT

Brief History of a Life

It is morning again in the old grey house.
Silence along the skirting-boards. Stillness

in the hall. Spirit-light. The boy-ghost
sits sullen, in pyjamas, top of the stairs,

fourteen steps down – where the carpet is frayed
and cobwebs frame the banisters; decades

down, metronome tock-tocks, and step, step, and step,
piano, the *Moonlight Sonata*, time! – faster soon:

Rondo a la Turka, allegro please – and now
that the walls and stairs have all dissolved, he still

sits, angry at the wet sheets, the dark, the unmanifested,
how the echoes of the 9th symphony's final chords

hang on the air before the thunder breaks.
And again it is morning in the old grey house...

A Mercian Hymn

from the Anglo-Saxon
Isaiah: Ezechias' Song

I said – now in my twilight years I will go down
to the roots of Sheol, and seek what is left to crown
the rest of my days. I will not find, I said, my Lord God
amongst the living. Nor will I look abroad
to any of the inhabitants of earth. My time
is lost to me. It has been stolen with my name
and folded away like a shepherd's tent. My life
has been snipped in pieces, as if a weaver's knife
had sliced it; and even then, still in my prime, I knew
misfortune. From dawn to dusk it is you
who have been completing me, from evening through
to dawn, like lions' teeth you have rushed to harrow
all my bones; from dawn to dusk it is you
who have been completing me.

                As a fledgling swallow
so will I cry to you; I sit and meditate on your words
like a dove. I have gazed so long heavenwards
my eyes have grown bleary; o Lord my Lord, see!
I am the butt of animosity, speak up for me,
when my words fail will you then answer as a lover
since you yourself are the cause? I will pick over
all my years in the bitterness of my soul.

                                    O Lord my Lord,
if life must take such a heavy toll, or if the onward
journey of my spirit must suffer always a new
warfare, it is you who must uplift me, it is you
who must give me life. See, in moments of peace
I find most bitterness, but you, o you, come to release
my soul that I may not perish. For you have thrown
all my sins behind your back. Hell on its own
will not confess to you, nor death praise you; those
who descend into the pit do not search its alleyways
for mercy. The living, it is the living rather
who will confess you, as I do this very day. The father
will make the truth clear to his children.

                                    O Lord my Lord,
keep us safe; and we shall sing our poems to the Lord
all the days of our life in the very house of the Lord.

Old Burningbush

I tramped the loose-stone cart-track into peatlands;
mist was hanging on the looped sienna hills,
clouds trailed, like smoke, along the mountain
and sunlight shifted in swathes across the lower slopes.
I find sustenance here, in cello-music rising to me
from the valley, falsetto notes of high-range skylarks
accompanying. For this is Achill Island. On Keem beach
a mountain stream carves out a miniature grand canyon
through the sand, yet all the world – in my green morning –
was accusation and the response was guilt – Yahweh
dragging me this way by the right arm and Yahweh
dragging me that way by the left, old Burningbush,
up-rearing pillar of cloud and pelter-down of brimstone.
Deep in the peat are secrets buried from the very
foundation of the world: bones of Abel, keys to the kingdom,
the cancer cure, the words of poems that would end
for always inhuman violence. There was a river that flowed
once out of Paradise, out from the island, and still flows –
on and on – down the rock-strewn valley of the world.

The Distant Hills

Goldfinch, this morning, were trapezing on the teasels,
    redpoll, siskin, shrike touched on the hazel tree;
under the whitesilk innocence of its blossoms
    the hawthorn's limbs are twisted in their growth.

I was sitting under the eucalyptus tree with the old books,
    Amos, Osee, Ruth. A slow mist had been fistling in
across the alder leaves and I could see the rushes,
    still as rust-haired soldiers, waiting. I know –

because I have not spoken – I have unclean lips
    and the roof of my mouth is turf-grit dry.
Jasmine, trailing across a wall, droops in an early chill,
    hangs limp and festering; when it sheens again

the scent will fill the dusk with sweetness the way honey swabs
    the mouth. Like birds, I am eating the seeds of praise,
of light and growth and seasoning, coming again to relish
    rainfall on a roof of galvanize and the silver

of sunshine following: epiphanies, offering a language
    to moisten the tongue with words. Now I watched
a tree creeper, like a mouse, work itself
    up the bark of the eucalyptus; its scimitar-bill drew out

the white-fat larvae: obedient, I said, to its nature
    as the distant hills take mythic colours from the haze.
I rose and closed the burning pages, content to touch on marvels
    and walk the earth with hurting, Genesis feet.

Rainbow

Already another year
is touching on high tide; winds
have been raising waves across the swollen meadow,

clouds grey and white and grey again
bunch up, like summer crowds on the slow road
home from the shore. Joy made covenant with me

these decades back, days on the riverbank
when trout responded to stick, twine and pin,
with woodbine fragrant after rain. I ran then, laughing,

from the scuttling forays of the white
farmyard geese. These later times I might expect
a flood of huge proportions, to purge us of the wars we wage

on the good earth, who have grown smart
with chemicals and missiles, though we hold to prayer
that love's unfaltering generosity might keep us safe – as Noah

and the remnants of all flesh
stood out one dawn on washed ground, smelt
the fragrance of woodbine after rain, and saw love

light up again
in all her promise
the dreary undersides of the clouds.

Go Down, Jonah

Jonah was an island. Surrounded on all sides
    by marshland. At the lake's edge he waded, watching
    reticent birds among the rushes: warbler, blackcap, coot;

sometimes an eel, biscuit and gold, wrapped itself
    familiarly about his heel, or out on the settled water
    a brown trout tippled the surface, moving the boy's

indolent ego to a lyric voice – I will name things, he thought,
    to hold them warm inside my life: the water rail,
    the phalarope, the knot. He suffered roll-call

in the lee of flowering escallonia – Seán, Seosamh, Tadhg –
    picked off by rote the long telling
    of eternal laws, with boys like him, restless and keen,

while the basic economies of the world were filling schoolbags
    with the undermining geographies of fact. Always
    he could hear the distant chuckling of the ever

unreasonable God: shift yourself, Jonah, to the mainland,
    prophesy of love and kind and service. He went down, rather,
    to stand aghast before the ocean; sometimes, he answered,

when I open my mouth to utter, no sound comes out.
    High tide was shuffling boulders about the strand,
    the black hag flew as if she would slip in under

any old door while crowds of rocks, skull-shaped and eyeless,
    held on the shore, apostle-mouths perpetually sounding.
    The wheatear stood and scolded from a white stone,

so small it could have been the knuckled heart of the big
    mountain, reduced to a pulse of sorrow over the rank,
    unfaithful country. Tell them, Jonah, their economies

are the great antithesis and the lie. Why me? he said; I whistle
  through the windy music of my words, I know nothing
  of their wars or politics. I will put words into your mouth,

God said, terrifying him. But he tried: *kelp*, and *octopus*, and *whale*,
  and said again – I have no words and your steadfast love
  undermines all justice. He watched a bug, the emerald shine

on its grey-black carapace, lifted his boot and crushed it. Wept. Then
  turned to be once more an island. A white stone. Prophet. And
  began again. Stuttering : *water rail, phalarope, knot...*

Classical Purple

Silence in the rhododendron wood is a laced
silence; dimness is netted by an always-drifting light,

earth's floor sweetened by the death of leaves and the rotted,
once-voluptuous magenta blossoms. Wood-pigeons

murmur to the world their plangent dove-gossip
and the western island mists dreep gently down,

persistent, fruitful and distressing. Time
has been burrowing deeply here, seeking the seductions

of sub-soil, the temple-building activity of moles.
Out on the road there comes the cacophonous

revving of a truck; in the ditch a rusted gate lies
old-tramp-lazy in a nest of ferns and fairy-fingers.

To stand in loneliness is like hearing, at its faintest,
an orchestra playing from a promenade across the bay.

The doves will fling themselves up all-sloggery,
wing-clapping, into air, leaving a nimbus of rain-drops

shaken from leaf and branch; everything making melody
within the pit. In all of growth and lethargy, there are

faults, halts, perversions and distractions; the weight of eucharist
often lingers bitter-sweet along the tongue – and yet!

one thing I will seek – the psalmist wrote – that I may live
in the house of the Lord all the days of my life.

Goldcrest

Of course they come back, the dead, because they are there,
just beyond our being, on the other side
of that nothingness we are scared of, because there is work to do,
on earth and in the heavens,

and because we haunt them. We hear the intricate
tock-tick-tock of the wound-tight
innards of creation: Laudate Dominum, Hagia Sophia, epistolary
symphonies of St Paul.

But our New God is not the Most High God :
he is Burning-bush and Whinny-hill and Furze-bloom; he is not
a gilt tabernacle bathed
in ethereal light – but goldcrest, flitting in the berberis

for a feast of insect while snow
flurries down through a wash of sunlight this out-of-season
Easter week. God
is not *not*, unchanging, unbegotten, ineffable, God is *is*. So I

– remembering days when the pink rose
rambled, and blackberries plashed purple kisses on my lips – find
contentment this side of nothingness, and being
ghosted by the presence of those I have loved, and lost.

Innocence

I am child of the island, son of its earth, spirit
of Atlantic waters, somepart wolf-soul, somepart

lamb, heather-breezes motherful on my skin, the ever-
sifting-settling sand-clay of its shore like the fretting

in my blood; island, contained, all ocean, mountain, cloud, I
ranging and loping to the overarching obedience

of planet and star, of darkness reaching over sea
to unknown places; soft-silted senses, edged by a landfall

density, my appetites easily assuaged, in the good air and rains,
the fern-world and morass of near-liquid and cold-blooded lives.

◊

I was innocent then, of God, of wickedness or grace, flew
with peewit, lurked with snipe, found the sacred names of things,

the embrace of light and darkness, the fatherful. Till
in preparation for the sacraments they told me sin, told

of the blood, the broken flesh of Jesus, of words mis-matched
to mask the truth, and I found it churlish of the Elders to drag

me in from the sun to a stained-wood pew and cramped
confessional, to tell the wildering trolls of my imagining;

scour, they said, the earthen things, become a dandelion seed
awaiting the Spirit's breath, be stable, stolid, be mainland.

A SMALL SALVATION

The Upright Piano

That summer the heavens opened;
days you'd think
Noah come again, eels
squirming in the streets and brown-water streams

harrowing the tarmac edges; birds
skimmed over the grasses, swallow, house-martin, swift;
starling flocks,
gossip-mongering in branches of the ash

lifted suddenly as one, though fractured,
sentence.
The coming by the house
of yet another downpouring of rain

sounded at first like the titter-tattering
legs of rats
racing across the stretched-taut skins
of tympani.

When they hoisted down an old upright piano
off the pier's edge onto a curragh
and rowed carefully out across the sound towards the island,
the rains came harder,

blotting out the world;
the boat lurched sideways into the reaching arms of a wave; piano
leaned lazily over and sank and now –
under the rough-cast gurgling cacophonies, the gripe-words

of the flowing past of waters – you will hear
the busy-fingered currents
perform a suite
of intricate and burble-delicate water-music.

The Ruined Meadow

Something of the reassurance of the seasons in it,
a tractor
out in the meadow, mowing; evening, high-sky blue,

and then the tractor going on through darkness,
headlights
sending fence-post shadows through the window;

they moved across the kitchen wall,
unholy shapes
shivering in a timeless silence. By morning

bales of light-green grass littered the shorn field.
Pigeon on the chimney-pot
hoo hwhoo hooed his love-call of sustained distress

echoing where the smooth presenter of this day's deadly news
spoke his own hoo hwhoos
into electric air. Syria, he said, the children... and stuttered

into silence. And then – billions of years in its fostering,
perched now
on the sheep-wire fence – there he was, robin, *spideog*,

with that engaging look-you-in-the-eye cockrobin-ness,
small chubby masterpiece,
created out of air and the plucky verve of spirit, plaything

of a fierce universe, reassurance, too,
in that sharp eye,
taking ownership of the mist, feasting in the tractor ruts.

Dawn to Dusk

Cattle – after a night of frost and stars –
appear to kneel in morning fog
and low a foggy music (the door
opening slowly onto commonage);

here – in the everyday year in which we live
and labour to effect a small salvation –
light shifts on towards night,
night towards light again.

Heron stands – motionless as a battered
parasol – among stones in the quiet shallows,
heron-eye wide and watchful;
noon-time sunlight will set ablaze

the green flaggers along the marshes;
angelus is tolling in the distance; now
is a silence containing in its breathing
the warmth of sap, of blood flowing.

Dusk – and heron stabs again – then
scatters water from its head, hoists itself
in cumbersome elegance and flaps
low over the pasture where I hear, at last,

its far, accomplished *craawrk*
as it heaves its sacred-spirit fuselage
(the door closing slowly on the mystery)
towards the high, the twilit trees.

Treasures

Out where the asking winds off the Atlantic
sieve through the wastes of bogland,

they have found the half-moon chased-gold lunula,
richness stored in the strong-box of clay,

humankind – even back then –
working to sustain a passionate kingdom.

I have been watching, on the island's coast,
a clustering of godwits, like a line of haymakers, raking,

astonished how they lift as one, suddenly,
and shear away, like the quick

impulsion of a thought. Down on the crumbling
sand-face of a headland cliff, they have found

the shattered wrist-bones of dead-born children
our godly gardens could not deal with,

where storms have been fingering by grain and grain, and play
the off-tune harp-song of human errors.

Along the foam of in-rushing slow-receding waves,
there is pearl-beauty in the rounded underbreast

of sanderlings, tiny birds that go running jiggety-tag
along the beach in quest of nourishment

from the flotsam of ocean, its treasure-hoard that yields, reluctantly
this earth's alleluia, its de profundis.

First Light

See again how, this morning – when you light the day's
first candle, when you settle yourself to quieten
the lingering tremors of last night's dreaming –
rehearsed words will mingle for a while with the small

flame-bud, hesitant; for a time you place yourself
in the presence of Who Is, listening. Blackbird,
on the backyard tree, is shivering his body
into startling song and a jet, high up and scarcely

audible, passes down along the stream towards Ithaca,
Babylon, or Samarkand; you will return to yourself,
let fall, repeatedly – into the well of quietness –

the name of the Source and Sustenance, and promise
you will not flee from the love offered. Then you leave,
the heart – like a peony – open again to vulnerability.

Parlement of Foules

... who said: Then let the air bring forth out of itself
all birds that fly...

The Nest

A dark world, of stench and cramp, of scramble,
up in the acute angle of the gable wall,
the jutting roof in its occlusion dumping dark
on dark; and then the beaks, yellow and livid

and big almost as the bone-fluff bodies, the blind
struggling for space, the crush and yawp for insects
to be stuffed in the gawping maws from above; until
that death of sorts, the adults urging, and the young

swift were out and tumbling, sickeningly, down; but
something in their being bloomed and there, suddenly,
was the whole unforeseeable earth and unrestricted sky,

the brash exultant rush of the body in instant mastery
of the elements, those spacious meadows of the air,
cloud-suffused blue fields, the azure pasture-lands.

Flycatcher

I watched through the wide-open window;
on the eucalyptus
a flycatcher, dink and dumpy, was darting out
and hovering, twisting its body back

to the sun-patterning blue-lit leaves; I heard
his busy *tsip-tsip* calling, times
I heard the bill snap shut on the sour-sweet giftedness
of an insect. Then it flew, beak filled,

in amongst the sharp-spiked branches of our elfin tree,
lone bush, haw in splendid bloom.
Shaddai, I said, how wonderful your works. A skylark

dribbled its high-pitched water-music on the sky
and in the meadow tall purple orchids stood in elegance
above the plumping grasses. I watched

the melt and flow of butter, the little-chopped sprigs of parsley
over the boxty bread, and knew myself, a while, appeased.
Until a magpie, potent and cackling, flew into the thorns
and the flycatchers came, flushed out, calling,

the bully-bird bursting back with small unfeathered flesh
fast in its beak; the green-and-purple gloss of its back
was the colour of slaughter, then it was gone, the flycatchers
circling, crying. Later I found the nest, woven –

with centuries of studying and instinct – out of fine moss,
one naked, torn fledgling lying in its mess. Angered,
I cried Shaddai! Unlovely! Why? all this... all this... and heard:

Made I the magpie so, and so the flycatcher,
the insect so? and are they mine, as you are mine, I theirs, and you?
But I stood sullen, grudge-heavy, greedy still for more.

Wren

This is not mere fidgeting inside
the hawthorn hedge: it is neat
house-work, building, quarter-inch
by quarter-inch, comfort of dry moss

secured with human hair, twig-
latticing, assembling – second by second –
the miracle of universe;
this is no brute beauty, no pride or plume,

it is flitting, eye-quick and instanting,
setting it out, singing it in pedantic
tock-tick and lock-snick, bird scarce visible

in the interstices of things, small but essential
to the thrust of seasons, the marrowing of the bones of being;
its nest the cosmos, its song the very Word.

Treecreeper

Which is part, too, of the universe story. The high eucalyptus, dead,
fallen to the teeth of a too-long frost, bark peeling away;
treecreeper, restless little bird, climber, true
                                    to its name and nature,

in short spurts, spiralling, husbanding; between bark and bole, the nest,
the tiniest, whitest rose-flecked, most perfect eggs, found pearls of being,
                                    hailstones
of potentiality, sea-pebbles shaped by universe at the very edge

of magnificent ingenuity, and the tree chosen, become again
                                    a sacred space,
                                    a sanctuary;
though fraught with danger: that sleek-wet rat, a honey-coloured Tom;

but, the Pauline epistles say, whether we live or whether we die
we are the Lord's, and in the treecreeper there is no sin.
In such a nest, once and for all, the word was hatched out into flesh.

White-Fronted

Flocks of the smaller birds
have been marauding across suburban gardens
this long-delaying winter: waxwings, long-tailed tits –
passing like flurries of snow before the breeze;

we wait for the white-fronted geese who will lift,
hundreds together, like a great umbrella opening
in the sky above us, to wheel quickly away, on that
appalling journey north; we will be left again

with the quarrelsome residents, the magpies, who patrol
our roofs and eve-chutes, chucking down
small clumps of moss on us in their hunt for grub.

So are we witnesses, to signs and wonders
though we may move, between the everyday and the sublime,
offering our small, stale crumbs, our shrivelling seeds.

Island of Saints

The whistle of a hawk
high above the lake; insistent green
of trees on the far shore,
stone-fed light of the low hills;

what has been lost
is the quiet of monks
held in the claws of suffering,
the rapture of harsh breast-beating

in consciousness
of sin. On the holy island
only the breeze
and the slow growth of moss.

The dark-brown waters tip with cream
where small waves foam and fly
like milk-white moths. We who come
are tourists, where the humming of bees

intersects with the holding back
of white deer,
near the standing of bishop-purple
digitalis. The saints are here,

Gobnait, Abigail,
Seán Ó Ríordáin dead and Seán Ó Riada dead,
old ways of prayer and an ancient language
falling off, though the music

lingers: quiet, and the sounds
of rainfall on the lake
reminding us of prayer, of time,
of the rhythms of gain and loss.

Coast

They were standing in the belly of the trawler,
big men in from the sea;
on the black-wet boards at their feet

boxes of fish, fat and slippery, their round eyes open,
dulled and bulging;
the men, in their orange wind-cheaters, their scaled and blooded

grey slaughtering-aprons, heisted the catch up
onto the quay
before the bulged eyes of the tourists, creatures,

out of their element, alien here, and cold
in biting air off the Atlantic.
But tonight, in the scents of onions and olive oil,

of pepper, tomatoes, lemons, warmly-lit rooms will be humming
to the savouring of blood-dark wine,
the taste of the charcoal skin of a black sole.

Best Western

The convent:
its neglected aisles, denuded transepts;
there were prayers here once, touching on how all human flesh
falls to the all of clay. Now in the walled garden,

apples and pears have grown small and hard as pebbles;
the sisters have found rest
in neat rows, a small white cross their portion, miniature roses
growing over. Only the gardener,

old red-eye stumbler,
tends to the ivies, burns dead leaves in a furthest corner;
the peacock lingers on, with the usual
tremendous difficulty in self-comporting,

rooting into the clay of the flower-bed,
that same iridescent blue of the neck, the wizardry of the crest.

Makes a fine Best Western now,
the trappings of bench and prie-dieu offering a quaint
titillation, trace of a vague
nostalgia. Hidden and soft-toned music

(like wallpaper humming)
in the lounge-bar, gourmet dining, deep-piled carpets
in each en-suite bedroom. Life, they will say,
moves on. The works of love renew

their ambience. The human heart
is manifold in its transitions. Still every night, in the walled garden,
you may hear the gardener's barrow
squeal its way along, gathering herbs, blue-purple damsons,

while the demoiselles of Santa Chiara
sway in choir, offering their high sweet voices to the breeze.

Eucalyptus

Two years the eucalyptus stood, dead
in its place, the death angel hesitant
to abandon it. I touched the bark, sorrow
a sap rising within me. The tree had been
inspiration, its yielding scent, its leaves
quivering, its arms housed for a swarm of bees,
crossroads for the snattering of goldfinch,
secret crannies for treecreepers, for flycatchers.
Its death was unspectacular, freezing where it stood
through a desperate winter. Held on, suffering
the indignities of despoliation. Skin shedding
in long, dun scabs, spoiling the lawn. Till I knew
the tree's love was an intensity I cherished
for all those years. Chainsaw, finally, against its skin
was a caress, guiding it to its fall – the slow
creak of its splitting, the splintering, like stained glass,
of its lesser branches, the dull thump of its trunk
against solid ground – all this a farewell, a plea
for forgiveness. The angel left with a sigh, the emptiness
that stood against the sky was a spirit lifted into air
and held close after the flesh's long dormition.

Hunger

I heard the barking of a fox,
urgent in the bitter-amber glow of the urban night; predator
through the small, untidy gardens,
she has perfected a steady loping, an easy watchfulness;

the glad and sorry facts of human living
are discarded packaging the fox-tongue probes, fox-eye
watches for. At the street's end
the traffic lights move on from red to green to amber,

nobody at this hour to heed them, these silent calls
to caution, to take care, survive.
In the sudden light the window throws, vixen looks up
from her hungers and is not stirred, she knows

the sound a back-door-click makes, knows too, perhaps,
that womanman, in its warm den, has its own hungers to satisfy.

A NEW TESTAMENT

Townland

Bethlehem: the village, and the townland,
crowded and expectant
like a fair day in Bunnacurry; in our dark cowhouse
there were snuffling sounds

and the warm, rich reek of cattle.
Bethlehem: Joseph and Mary standing,
wide eyes fixed on one another,
the whimper of a boy-child in between; brown earth outside

was frumped and sodden
under the slow breathing of mist. A harsh half-moon
shivered on the frosted road
down to the Bunnacurry church, and we, children,

bundled ourselves tight
in winter coats, our breathing forming angel-shapes
on the biting air. It was just a birth; one
out of millions that had come before, of millions

that would come after; this one birth
neither a beginning, nor an ending; a turning-point
merely, though shading all that went before, all
after, tossing the rags and peelings of time into the uncertain

texture of eternity. Bethlehem: stars
above the caverned escarpment. Crib and candle-light
in Bunnacurry chapel, where we knelt
awed by festival, by the silence surrounding, by the animals.

The Whole World Over

Budapest

I see him, mariner Jesus, walking on corrupted
waters of the Danube while down in silted depths
lurk the unexploded bombs of lately wars; I walk out,
hand in hand with the poem, crossing on the high

redemption bridge, to earth corrupted by tar and concrete,
where down in the darkly shiftless soil words crawl,
eyeless and eager. Between sleep and day, light
and black, I grow conscious of compelling truths –

but something in the ego-wassailing of flesh compels me
back to comfort, and something in the slippery
eel-mud of the mind eases towards sleep, though always

Jesus plods on over all the corrupted waters
heading for the unforgiving hill, for his piercing
cry of forgiveness out-into-the-outraged world.

Dark Mother

Something, Yeshua-of-grace, about the guard-dog
wagging the stump of his tail to every traveller;
about the courage to be unshaken, lone in the dark kitchen,

smoke from damp peat catching in her throat.
That her dull reiterated labours – from the black kettle
to the washtub by the back door, from the hens

scratching in the yard-dirt, from the washing-line back
to the caterpillar-chewed cabbage – may not be in vain.
You are wisdom, way beyond our ways; yet you too

left a mother in tears, and there was talk,
in the oil-light, of an absent father, of work
in far-distance exile, Liverpool Birmingham Glasgow;

till she sat, lone in the morning kitchen,
cold in the absence of sons. You, Yeshua-of-grace,
walked in your own sadness, suffering flesh,

skiffed a chisel against your finger, drawing blood,
dropped a clutch of eggs – be, Miryam's son, emigré, be
joy of her joy, pain of her pain, stillness of her stillness.

Visitation

Sometimes when I wake, wolf-hour, the dearth
between high-tide of darkness and the return,
I will question benevolence: I will ask –
what of the all-at-once love-words of annunciation?

At noon, near the eucalyptus tree, I will wonder:
what of the wrung-out cries of a man
writhing in agony, nailed through wrists and midfeet
to a rough-hewn timber? The agonies we suffer:

what of them if it is all pointless? It was – *primo tempore* –
a harried journey Miryam made from Natzrat to Yerushalayim:
a girl, scarcely woman, three months pregnant, hurried
through desert heat, past ribald nomads, bandits, wanderers –

to come to the hill country of Ein Karem, Spring
Vineyard, violets opening, the terraces ripe, the trees –
life coursing through seed-pod, vine-flower, nest.
It was Spring, too, for us, the pilgrims, climbing;

that day we were old hawks on hot thermals, grateful
for ice-cream, coffee, and still yearning for the world's
perfecting, grieving at the everywhere of human depredation.
Who will hold on to a deep-down gracefulness

under the scum and scumbling; who imagine still
the jubilant fullness of bells at noon as they ring out
over the valleys, and the wonder in an old woman's voice
when she called out a hearty greeting – Miryam!

Blood

I was sitting in the scullery, watching mother
peel carrots into the rough-stone sink;

the carrot-skin came as a smooth curlicue off the knife,
the carrot-flesh aristocratic;

then the parsnips, and 'pshaw!' she said, scraping dirt
off a knobbly workaday shape; the vegetable, peeled,

was ghost-grey flesh naked. Outside
under the whitesilk innocence of the blossoms

hawthorn limbs were contorted in their growth.
Mother was humming her no-rhythm no-tune hum;

I thought of her as a sonata taken apart
and the notes scattered, when, suddenly, her fingers

slipped; she held up, silenced, in surprise, her hand;
I saw drops of such vivid red and heard them

plop slowly down into the sink. And I thought
of the bright boy Jesus, just my age, of Mary

humming her busy-woman hum in the sunyard,
and wondered if the child of his woodman father

(should the precise chisel slip) was brave enough not to cry
as a bubble of blood grew bigger on his finger-tip.

Pulse

Catwalks of goldfinch on the branches, in a fashion-parade
of colours, of party-feather boas; now, in dusklight,
the breeze is snuffling in the high poplars

in that gentling hour you stand, before sleep,
under the moon-sliced-in-two, while above you, you surmise
the snow-feather wonder of swans, the heart-beat effort

of wings in flight; and higher still the steady process
of a satellite moving to the same heart-beat.
Light from a window far across the valley goes suddenly

out; you know that, further off, in the tumulus at Newgrange,
swallows fledge down deep in the throat of earth,
preparing – on the marvel of their wings – a summer solstice...

Nonetheless, in the fleshly heart, there is again
news of the massacred laid out on a concrete floor
in Syria, rose-petal stains on the walls, and you turn away

to bow, a moment, in the quietness of prayer, in the ragged
shadow of the eucalyptus, while the tender wall of darkness
behind your eyes is edged for a moment in blood-light.

The Side-Aisle

I was thinking of the eucalyptus, the raw nights
of snow, the prolonged stillness

of frost-sheened days; of the crack
of an old branch, the sluggish crying of a fox

far over snow-bound hedgerows; in these
I had sensed communion

and though the eucalyptus fragrances
disappeared, and the whisperings of presence,

though the flesh of the bark
fell off in strips and browned to a thick parchment

like Qumran scrolls – I would speak of its life's completion
in the long sigh it made as it fell

all of its heavy length along the ground;
as I have sat here, watching – in the brass-and-candle

city loneliness of a left-side aisle – a distraught father
lifting his brawling baby out into the light;

and watching, too – as a bell sounded its ponderous urging –
an old woman go scuffling her heavy frame forward,

and I could see the whittled tongue
offered, as though famine-fraught, here where I

answer, have answered, year upon year, the call
of the host, savouring that wood-chip taste

of the bread and straining always
towards fellowship.

The Wall-Clock

Out in the hallway our morning coats
steamed after rain; around the dark-stained,
ochre-dull rough walls

the charts and histories of the journey,
skulls of primitives, stone implements,
the beards and weapons

of gesticulating prophets.
A wall-clock, sand-coloured face
framed in chestnut,

brass pendulum and heavy weights moving
too slowly, hung ugly on the classroom wall.
Lessons in the ways of Christ

were gobbets of seed-cake indigestible;
the Brother, in dark-brown habit, stalked
and stormed and wielded,

there was little light, less warmth. But something
rooted in me, some Jesus-thing lingering yet, almost
against my will.

Now I form part
of a diminishing comradeship, who make our way, Sundays,
under the great, hushing trees,

to rummage again through rites and mysteries.
I kneel, contented with what remains
after those deckled years:

peace before glazed windows, peace
among benevolent spectres who have stepped along beside me;
while the beloved lately dead

are hymning their way out of darkness
into the saffron-bright, clarified daylight
of their all-knowing.

The Downs, The Cedars

I shift across suburban territory, past the cute
be-ribboned gardens, four-by-fours
discreet and ostentatious, ego-sheen off chrome
and alloy. I have been enquiring after
suburban Jesus, if he has turned in off the avenue,

if he walks here, hesitant, without authority,
through Grove and Heath, the Downs, the Cedars,
leafleting where he can; to know if the feral cats
come chafing themselves against his trouser legs
as he steps cautiously round dried-up dog-turds;

doors closed, alarms, no junk mail, no
mystery. What news, then, of the inner life? The postman
whistles, bin lorries clank… politicians, thieves…
and the Christ still labours on towards Calvary,
the heavy crossbeam pressing on his shoulders.

Letter from East Anglia

for Dr Rowan Williams

Dear Pilgrims,

The light is a late autumn light, there is a certainty
of frost; trees – ash and maple and eucalyptus –

stand in their pastel colourings, the smaller roads
are damp after last night's star-rife sharpness

and will not dry out in these short, slatternly days.
Chill winds off the North Sea, East Anglia, cut to the bones,

skin is ragged, like shredding sails. In Norwich, in Julian's
modest cell, nobody comes calling, dry leaves hustled

by the breeze outside make the softest sounds. Candles,
and coins dropped into the wall-safe, are a pleading

that every manner of thing, on the journey, might be well.
In the market-square, a woman at her stall – herring

in from the North Sea – scrapes fish-scales and blood
from the boards with a killing-knife; Julian said –

Jesus is motherly, comforting in his homelyhood. We

have come on windy side-roads through the spreading pastures
of the Giddings, pilgrims, moving like flocks of foam

blown upon the sea. Small red apples scent the air
and feed the shadowed ground below; silence

holds the greening gravestones in a gossipy
lean-together in the church yard, while at times

the doves make mess among the pews and kneelers;
schoolchildren from the parishes, kneeling against

Ferrar's table tomb, sketch the peaked bell-tower
of George Herbert's church.
                                        Dear pilgrims:

   En-route to Little Walsingham, step in a while
   to the Slipper Chapel,
   and say some words to the Saxon Lady
   Richeldis de Faverches;

   there has been a breakthrough here into the impossible;
   Annunciation Window
   is a 40-voice motet in blue, from the dark of night
   to the whiter blue of Mary's robe;

   even the moon – announcing its scimitar-shaped *yes* in white –
   is filled with crêpe-de-chine of blue;
   what more there is of white is the sceptre Joseph lily,
   a dove's flight that sets the black on fire;

   the startling, stalwart angel – who blows in from the west –
   does not seem out of place, place
   that is chapel, that has been poorhouse, cowshed, forge – now
   locus for dreams

   and barn for the dance of possibilities – for the raising of a chorus
   against the crowding in of sorrows,
   a shoreline for the launching of the imagination
   into the blue beyond of hope.

   Listen! the still-young girl in question hears her name
   spoken out, with feeling,
   in the strangest tongue, hears words announcing nothing on
                                                      this earth
   will ever be the same again.

Pilgrims:

In Ely, shop-window canopies crackle in the wind,
like distant gunfire from a battle out on the North Sea.

The nave, in this great Ship of the Fens, is a redwood
forest of all-Saints, all-Souls, holding the history

of our salvation: Oak of Mamré, Jesse Tree, and Calvary...
In the Lady Chapel, the angel's words of greeting: his *ave*, his

sé do bheatha, his *je vous salue*... were words that made as one
the raw earth of our scrublands and the heaven of our hopes;

in the intertestamental sunshine you can hear the Virgin's
high shout *Magnificat!* and the long, reiterated litanies, humankind's

polyphony of pleas and pleading. A field-hawk, evening,
soars in ease over trim and dusk-lit small-towns of the shire.

ACCORDING TO LYDIA

According to Lydia

Cock-Crow

It was soon after dawn and he was out already,
raw and impatient, for we could hear his axe
splitting wood, the first dull dunts, then the quick
rupturing sound, its echo against the roosters' calls;
there was strength and such assurance in the sound
the village came to itself with a morning confidence;
the thousand-year-old olive stumps resisted stanchly,
but he would later polish the wood to a perfection
smooth to the thumb. By noon he'd pause, listening
to the laughter of young girls busying themselves
among the vines. Then, in the afternoon loafing-hours,
he would slip away to some hidden wilderness
alone, as if fruits of earth and toil were slight. A shadow
would darken the woman's face watching from the doorway :

Bedrock

Wilderness. We heard first about locusts and wild
honey; then, demons and beasts. Sheer absences, no
water. Shade. Comfort. The sun so fiery that the low hills
shimmer like a mirage. There are cool, sheltering places,
occupied. Easy to believe in demons, so little sound
there the mind hums. By day the burning, by night
the crackle of frost; thudding stillness of the heart, admitting
wisdom, dust-awareness; immured in desert nothingness
and the struggle with the mind. Opening to loneliness,
to the holiness of the unresponding; garnering strength
against the worst that noon can do, or the trailing moon;
dying to flesh-hungers, earning a certainty
that washed him through with tenderness, that raked
spirit and flesh to a sheer, uncompromising love :

The Binding

The lake's edge – generation after generation
depending, shallow at the shores, bronzewater, gold;
millennia of shells, patterned dull and gay, becoming grit –
profound, a harvest, what's left of innumerable deaths.
They have drawn the boats up onto the grass, and sit
examining the nets; the human heart, they know, is forged
out of such bindings, such husks, at the very lip
of wilderness. This day, out of a sky so bright
it chafes like silver, they hear the high-pitched cry
of a swooping sea-eagle ripping the air. The man –
in mulberry-coloured robe and leathern sandals – has passed
down along the margins towards the boats; at once
there is disturbance, a sharp kerfuffle at the lake's edge
and the brothers, without a backward glance, forsake the shore :

Kfar Nahum

Beyond the village, willows, scrub grass, small waves
frivolously fingering the shore; warm breeze under grey,
scarce shifting, clouds; the day lifeless, and everyday
ordinary; a fishing-boat drawn up onto stones,
no shore-birds visible; noon, as if the world had
paused, uncertain, waiting. In the crumbling synagogue
craftsmen and fishermen sat, bemused, the stranger
standing before them, reading, and expounding; as if he bore
quietness in his bones in spite of the earthed resonance
in his voice; the authority, the unaccountable wisdom
that had been concealed somewhere in the Torah scrolls,
the mourners, the merciful, the hungry. Puzzlement
among them, here and there a muttering anger. Words,
as ours, but new, and other. A man like us. Unlike. But like :

Disturbances

By sunset, in Kfar Nahum, he had drawn to himself
many of the broken, crazed and trodden-down,
the undesirables, the pariahs and the freaks;
the space between gate and lake was a market-field
of clamour, pleading, incredulity and tears. Soon
he was exhausted. A yellow moon
hoisted itself slowly above the village, and a crow,
lifting in dudgeon out of the roost, called a loud
craw! to the clouds. By now, we were unsure of it,
what had happened, for something difficult
was insinuating itself within the stepped-out limits
of our life, but we knew there would be consequences,
grave. It was owl-night, the bird calling out 'who? who?';
can what is broken be whole again, what's crooked straight :

The Flowering

That night we lit lamps everywhere, outside, within,
on grass and pathway, down to the shore; he sat on,
all light and shadow, his words gathering radiance
and darkness into their texture; we lived a while in an island
of being, apart, and unmanageable; and oh! the strangeness:
a cock crowing, bright-winged moths singeing themselves
against the flames; smoke from the oils sometimes
itched the eyes but we stayed, startled when he said: *your
sins are forgiven!* and no-one, there and then, doubted it –
we thought of our blessed YHWH; we thought of the stone
heads and torsos of gods in the city set on their shaky
pedestals, and the night swelled; as if the raw green stem
of the Pentateuch were about, latterly, to open into
a great red wound, like the high and blossoming amaryllis :

Demons

It takes a lifetime to cast demons out;
you struggle with them, you, demoniac, you, unclean,
they throw you down, you howl inside, you get
up again, you have to. Lest they destroy you. He
touched them, lepers, too, their sores, their bandages,
their dead eyes. He would take all burdens on himself.
Thirsted and hungered have we, for such as he, to enter
into the soul's holding. I have found, down in my heart,
there is a sphere so still, so silent and untouched
it is pure as the snow-topped summit of Hermon
glistening in the distance. He came, gathering them all to table,
the manic, the castaways, the hobbled (we thought him mad)
and there was laughter, and quiet and – I tell you this –
peace where never there was peace, nor laughter ever :

Table

I need to tell of this, I need to set it down –
how he brought them in with him, and how they grinned
at the shaken host; servants, with disdain, offered water
for their hands and feet but the stranger knelt and
helped them: the beggars, the bedraggled, and the whores;
they reclined on cushions at the rich man's table: who did not
eject them, offering lamb and artichokes and goat's cheese,
wine and pickled fish and pastries soused in honey; they
asked for barley bread and barley beer. The stranger broke
and dipped the bread and passed it to them, told them jokes
and stories of lost sheep and prodigals and wheat seeds scattered
against the wind. It was, the host adjured, a ghostly meal, touched him
with joy and bitterness, this kingdom rife with casualties –
but it was I, he said, who found I was immured in poverty :

Samaria

Jacob's well, Shechem, route of nomads, revolt, crusade...
of people toiling down valleys of silence into exile: she
drawing near – heart torn by love-failures – to the source now,
the sustenance. The stranger, waiting; out of exodus and genesis
with demanding words. Between them, issues of time, of history,
the depths of the iced-over, petrified heart. 'I thirst': who, then,
is keeper of the soul in need: he, or she? Between them, between
past and future, the clarity of water in the moment of its
giving, words echoing beyond the sound of words, beyond clanging
of consonant, bird-call of vowel, how the heart, in its taut holding,
wants to yield, to the presence, the immediacy. She, later,
returning home, stumbles, her pitchers full. He
stays, on the ridge of stone, staring down into the deep
till the moon brightens, down there, in the uttermost darkness :

Papyrus

The word, I have discovered, is food for my surviving,
this need to lay down words on strong papyrus, in strait
and patterned lines, hints of love and yearning, and now
this penchant towards sorrowing, for memory is un-
certain, inaccurate, and, like waters, fluid. Words of Yeshua
who sought to slip away, before dawn, to a desert place, to touch
his source and sustenance. For after all, after that mid hour,
my life will not be what it was; what, then, had happened? The word
existence seemed to shift, as boulders shift in a quake, the straight
line of living twisted back upon itself in a kind of anguish,
what we had accomplished suddenly became undone, the
comfortable dark was now backlit by a more aggressive fire –
for he had stood, tears on his cheeks, before the sealed tomb;
he called: and there was a death-silence: I heard a hum

of insects, somewhere the sharp howl of a jackal, an echo
out of Lethe and in the heat of noon my body chilled;
slowly, they unsealed the tomb, stood at its gaping mouth
mute in darkness; the sisters clutched each other, terrified.
He emerged, slow, slow, shrouded in white cotton, like a great
woodcock with folded wings, body camouflaged in snow,
and it was I who called, out of a living hope within me,
fly high! Lazarus, fly! But he stood still: perplexed, perhaps
blinded by the sun, when the sisters moved to him, and the crowd
astounded, cried with a shrill ululation, like flocks of startled
shore-birds until he stood, freed, and moved towards Yeshua
like a lover stepping out in exaltation. I understood there is no
such thing
as the ordinary world, that words themselves are not
transparent, and I became, just then, afraid of this man of men :

Mediterranean

Came that day on the beach; Yeshua stood a long while
and spoke, of love, of mercy, of tenderness; and my spirit
sang again. We grew hungry. There he was, frying fish over stones,
with garlic, oil, fresh bread, and I could not figure
from where came all that food. There were sea winds, and each
morsel that we ate spoke benevolence while the ocean, behind us,
murmured its assent. He had his place now in my heart, no, it was
even deeper than the heart. We had come for pleasure, what we took
was the scent of the sea, a sense of comfort mixed with dread,
the sunset pink of flamingos flying over. I remember the new port,
breakwaters, the Roman galleys, new economies; the stranger –
Yeshua – had taken spittle on his fingers and touched the eyes
of a blind man; but Yeshua had mentioned fear and we saw,
beyond the grasses and wild flowers a small group, hostile, gathering :

The Garden

Dusk – the sun going down – threw long shadows across
the ground. He appeared, coming from the valley, and collapsed
on the hard earth; somewhere a bird sang, though the word
'chuckled' came to mind. I remembered Genesis: the Lord God
walking in the garden, time of the evening breezes. An hour
passed; the world darkened further; up in the city
lights flickered. I thought I heard sobbing, even a scarcely
suppressed cry. He rose, and moved, stumblingly, back
towards the wall; I heard voices, protestations. Then he came
to fall again, scrambling on earth as if his bones were fire
and though I sensed rather than saw his body, he was distorted
like limbs of the olive trees. I heard weeping; I heard fingers
scrabbling against ground. Weakness, and failure; embarrassing.
Relief to see the flare of torches coming this way from the city :

The Viewing

When he was harried out to be jeered at, blood-
ugly, rag-scraggly, filthy with sores, I knew
he must be guilty and I was ashamed. He could
scarcely hold himself erect, they jostled him,
there was blood congealing on his face, his
fingers, even on his naked, blistering feet. He had no
hope, he was already stooped amongst the dead.
Like a fool he stayed silent, stubbornly so, though
words could not save him now. This was degradation
before the people, who mocked his agonies, his death,
the ultimate humiliation, for even rats
will creep away to die, in private, in a dark
corner. We knew now that his name would be
forgotten, left with his corpse in merciful oblivion :

Hill of Skulls

(i)

I stood on the slope, at a distance from the other women;
it was done on the Hill of Skulls, dread place, to discourage
thought; high posts planted, waiting for the cross-
branches, the flower, and the fruit, where the dead earth
was rusted over with spilled blood; a little aside –
though within eye-shot – from the city's bustle and indifference.
Miryam, for it must be she, stood propped between strength
and failure, determined mother to the last. I had dreamed
he would put an end to violence. The big iron nails
were not the worst, though the heavy hammer-blows
shuddered the earth and shuddered my heart – it was the body
writhing in agony, chest strained beyond the possible at each
in-breath, out-breath, it was how humankind spits hatred
against its own, the tender-hearted, innocent, the children – but

(ii)

it's how things are, the soldier said, and will always be.
The moments passed, each one dragging as an hour; I tried
prayer, but to whom, or to what? The sky darkening, the groans
lengthening, the screams… He was burning. Near us the cackling
magpies. In the sky, the vultures. The way, he had said,
the truth, the life – is the way death, then? Life, the urgencies
only of the body? And truth, what is truth? His blood
mingling on the earth with blood of the contemned. Love
the final casualty. Clouds blackened; hot winds
blew in across the hill, shadows were dancing wildly
amongst confused noises. He cried out, though rarely. My
tears were silent, copious. I heard a distant, drawn-out
thunder. After such hours he screamed out, died; as if
he had exhaled, with his last breath, all the light and

life of the world. Thunderstorms as they took
him down, as I hurried through the streets people
were staggering by, like ghosts. I never felt so
much alone. That was the most muted evening,
night was black and long and I armed myself about
with fires of spitting olive-wood; in the laneways skulked
furtive shapes; I clung, desperately, to the supposed
mercy of time; words had lost essence and would spill
like hot grease. How could the world know he had lived, how
could the word love be redefined? Everything unfinished, all
undone. But I had inks, formed out of soot and oil and tears
and would carve deep in the papyrus. I remember – back then
on the mountainside – he had said: those of singleness of heart
will be blessed, for it is they who will see God :

Sunrise

So clear we had not grasped it: in the giving away of life
you find it. Soon after dawn I was leaning on the stone walls
of the vineyard out beyond the city. There was a well, timbers
covering it; I heard the wood rattling; there was a man
stooping over, reaching for a drink; he saw me, called out
something, waved, and was gone. Tricks of the light, I thought,
the sudden wing-claps of doves distracting. I stayed, fingers
worrying the clay between the stones. I had not even
waved back. Bright this early and I imagined the valley
singing softly. The intimacy of grape-flesh, I thought, the skin
peeled off, the dark wine waiting. The mind can find itself
so foolish, hoping for too much. The quickening of a heart
urgent against grief. Or urgent towards unutterable
joy. And I stood there, stood, baffled again by this one life :

The Turning

After the killing, there was no hope left, nowhere
to turn. We abandoned the city, wondering if we might
get somewhere. Sat, disconsolate, by the river, knowing
how goodness appears and is vanquished before it is
clasped. Wondering if there is a way for mortal beings
to start over. Someone, walking the same path, may offer
wisdom, and insight. Becomes, in the nonce, mediator
between place and non-place, life not-life, death and
not-death. The day advancing, our steps more sprightly,
we would hold to light against the nightfall. That someone...
Logs blown to flames in the hearth; dried fish, olives, figs
and honeyed wine; the ready warmth of love, the torn hands
blessing and breaking bread. What the blood had known
known now in spirit and for truth. And so we turned :

Lydia

I fear onslaughts of foolishness before the end,
the loss of wonder when the mind cools, the wine
ordinary, the bread bread. Do not fear, he said, only
believe. I work to keep the heart open, glory in the once-fire
that will be ash, in reason beyond reason. I work to cherish
the variegated birdsong, the damson flowers blossoming
when they will. That I may ever overflow with Yeshua,
as a jug will overbrim with a wine both sweet and bitter.
I know I will meet him again, the raw wounds of humanity
on his flesh. I remember the sea's edge, when, late evening,
he spoke from the fishing-boat anchored just off-shore: See
and hear as a child, he said, that the deaf hear and the blind
have their eyes opened, the lame walk and the dead rise again
and blessed is the one who does not lose faith in me.

VIOLIN CONCERTO

Constellations

There is no word for the newspaper page
on which father
cut the head and gutted out the innards of the twelve
mackerel he had caught,

wrapping the package tight with twine
and the brown blood showing through; no words
for the sound the swift will make
swooping through the high narrow streets of old Siena,

where we had visited with the saint, Caterina Benincasa,
whose spoken love for Yeshua
made every step of the way to heaven into heaven.
They have shaped the letter W of the five-star Cassiopeia,

giving words and letters to the impossible
though when we gazed towards them we could name but three:
Bathsheba, Deborah, the Magdalene.
In the dream, we were sitting, Yeshua and I, comfortable

within the breadth of dusk,
out on the patio by the swimming pool, both of us enthralled
by the savour of a chilled Anjou rosé wine,
with occasional sips of a sparkling

San Pellegrino mineral water, chewing on green-salt
roasted pistachio nuts.
Scents from night-breathing flowers – jasmine and buddleia –
out in the wild meadow, came over like repeated

grace-notes. And we were listening to the Mendelssohn
violin concerto, and then,
after a pause for silence, Max Bruch, the violin, the number one.
Again we sat, contemplative and at peace,

for what words could there possibly be. Wordless too, both of us,
attending to the mosaic of stars that moved
through Bruckner's sumptuous symphony
number eight, Yeshua's left hand deftly conducting everything.

A Mosaic

I have grown a little laggard now, a more practised
postulant for eternity;

body (as it always has)occupies my attention –
its sometimes frosty

relationship with spirit – taking care on stairs and escalators,
nervous of slip and hip.

I remember setting out, on the drab-green bus,
to leave the Island,

unwilling to elbow clear a space on the fogged-up window,
lest courage fail, the clink

of the conductor's ticket-machine the final
lock-click of a door. So have I lived

in bemused communion with the crinkled skin of language,
the grace of love, given and received. Now,

from the brightly-lit galleries of mercy,
so many faces of the lost watch out at me

through sheer
cut-crystal glass, soft-focused faces and inveigling,

that I think of the heady fragrances of hyacinths,
how they drain to the sweet

odours of decay. And shall I have – after it all –
realised anything of consequence,

or added one emerald tessera
to the star-floored dwelling-place of Yeshua incarnate?

Like Shooting Stars

The elms, after the plague that passed across them,
stand like distorted crucifixes,
derelict of purpose; now it is Easter, our Yeshua
dwells in promise, rising to light

out of the rigor mortis of stained-glass perfection;
now we will live a while
in the divine tenderness, the intensity of what is beautiful.
Moths bloom, like stars, otherly and aloof –

hawk-moth, swallow-tailed, the feathered thorn –
sadly collectable, as David stole Bathshcba;
they are fragile, like faces of the lost,
ready to filter into dust, and have appeared from nowhere,

hosts of them, testing the window-panes
as if merely looking in, unwilling to intrude. The dead,
in the delicate memories we have of them,
flare up so quickly, like shooting stars, and disappear.

Bodies of the moths tick like grandpa clocks
against our world a while, wings lustrous with coloured dust,
here from a distant darkness,
seeking – and offering – reassurance: come!

come to the light! let your life flare
into love, let it glow with intense and steady passion.
The moths emerge, passionate in name and essence,
like prophets

who set themselves on fire before us : one
short sizzle and whoosh, and all that is left is black ash
– clinging a while, shivery wisps of a dream –
leaving us to relish beauty, the brilliance, and the loss.

Tesserae

We, old folk, have turned, like the Magdalene,
scared to believe, fearful of unbelief. At Eucharist

sometimes we wonder about the dream
of bodily resurrection, hearing the diminishing

echoes of a grand old opera, as we shift along
on the pallid side of desire;

for we live now
with the most primitive demands of body, here still

by the grace of Yeshua,
still part of the on-going cosmic journey, almost

too stiff to kneel, in such uncomfortable pews,
sharing with two elderly sisters, shrunken

into mirror images of one another,
who walk a little way apart, cherishing small resentments;

some of us wield silver-headed walking-sticks, sing the hymns
a little hoarsely, just a shade off-key;

yet we have gathered in our time
such treasurable loveliness, who have stood together

scarcely breathing beneath the sand-silver constellations
in a warm and ebony sky, have shared

such vigour and desire that we have pushed a little forward
the frequented trails and sign-posts, our fortune

compressed in purse and deep vaults of the mind,
hurt by the racing past of time, tremendously content.

As the Stars of Heaven

They are out there in immeasurable darkness,
the ghosts – multiple as stars –
of the beloved and the lost, *all the fire-folk sitting in the air*
and, choiring without sound,

they move in the soft foundations
of our dreams. There is a tenderness we sense in them,
Bathsheba, Deborah, the Magdalene,
that they are reaching towards us, easing us in our yearnings.

Storm force ten off the western coast, the possibility
of a trawler swamped by monstrous waves, bodies pitched
off deck into roiling seas; this
the romp of powers beyond the human hold, awareness

that body and will may be incapable before such
brute perfection. On the Island's shores, mothers wait,
calling out to Yeshua who walked the waves,
small berthed boats up-shaken in the harbours, storm-winds

sweeping words away
while the heart is juddering in distress. They are out there,
ghosts of the prophets and the hosts, presences of an immense
and active happiness, urging our part

in the labouring of the universe towards fruition;
and Hopkins, in his cell in Beuno's, suffering lightning and lashèd rod,
calls on Him, *ipse, the only one, Christ, King, Head...*
While we, morning, palates

satiated sweet from that same tasted Christ,
have still no words to tell we have grown close
to the beloved lost, as we walk out towards the light,
slight figures, under the great stilled oaks and the sycamores.

THE WORLD IS CHARGED

Fly-Tying

I watched him, hooked over the kitchen table,
    the instruments of his heart's desire
ranged before him: tweezers, dubbin, vise;
    materials – feathers, threads, fluffs and beads;

such colours, amaranth, saffron, taupe;
    the delicacy, like down of thistle, like catkin-milt;
the hidden hooks, to dazzle a watery eye, and all
    worked between thick and nicotine-stained fingers.

He opened out his folding wallet, his treasury of flies,
    richness beyond delight, all beautiful and murderous.
I, too, inveigled, though on a lesser scale, in my way
    was searching the world's presence for its pulse and throb;

the vegetable garden, after rain, yielded its lush
    pink-red worms I gathered in to his old tobacco tin.
Dusk, and he was wading into the lake, he curled
    the fleshly-coloured line onto the water, the chosen flies

vivid as if they lived. I, with stump-rod, twine and worm
    sat by the river pool, watched the cork, dreamed
and – impatient at his patience – slapped at midges.
    Who has long gone into the anima mundi, rest

for the soul, the spirit-wallet filled with all good things,
    peace for the flesh from the flesh's urge, to be and to be
more than it may be here: clay, and thread, bright
    gaud and hook, and subsequent disappointment.

The Village Schoolroom

She stood, harsh mistress, declaiming to the girls
the catechism of their living;
they sat in desks, frayed cardigans and skirts,
their boots grime-cracked,

– somewhere between ignorance and lowliness –

suffering the naked present; she chalked – the words
scraping across the board –
the seven precepts of her Church. On the brown-drab wall
the pendulum of a big clock

– articulating, as they, the tedium of the world –

swung in a brown monotony, following the on-going
rhythm of the earth;
on the window-sills, jam-jars offering the ditch-side tadpoles,
the yellow irises, told

– distinctive and unrepeatable, as the girls are –

of the movement of the seasons. Sin, she admonished them,
comes from our first parents
who cast their guilt on us, and we live in sin and wickedness.
Mother, dead these decades,

I wish for you the radiance of eternity.

The Turning

Almost solstice; on an ice-blue sky the fluffed-wool
dissolving trail of a jet, stitching, unstitching; to-night
there will be stars, sharp as broken ice-glass
and small birds sheltering somewhere, in the earth's care;

here love evolves, through the small events and the remarkable;
you, in the garden, vivid in red windcheater,
your rubber gloves – one yellow, the other blue – as you deal
in clay and mulch, lift the tubers of this late summer's

dramatic dahlias – the bitter-lemon star, the all-hallows-red
Bishop of Llandaff – and lay them out in knotted sausage-shapes
in the *tigín* to dry; you turn, a moment, towards me, and smile;

the house is quiet, where I sit inside the window, watching,
hearing the vole-like scritch and scratch of my biro, as it turns, turns
to work at the daunting, cosmic whiteness of the page.

for Ursula

The World is Charged

I was startled by the squawk, the simultaneous
long-tailed and spread-winged half-spectacular half-dive

of the cock-pheasant, his wattles, his bronzed body
up over the hedge; and see! there! the Japanese anemone,

pea-green heart within a scatter-ring of gold; and here –
humbler still, and local – see the mares-tail weed

and the quick reaching of the briars, note, too, how the tiny
pimpernel persist along the driveway, from the red gate

to the front door. Astonishment, from heart to eye to ragwort,
from there to woodlouse, eucalyptus, owl, and on to Sirius

and the Plough... And we have been, years, she and I,
walking by fields where generations lived and loved,

have laboured and have disappeared – with their sheds
and implements and cattle – into the deep, where they stay

resonant in their silence, their poorer cottages crumbled
into liqueur of rose hip, dust of nettle, knowing that we too

will be with them, alive and loving in the warm light
that still persists, hereabouts, and everywhere, and forever.

The Great Fire

He was, in the mathematics, in the catechism,
quicker, and more fluent;
we were brothers, carefree together for a time,
and lived where the rains wash in from the Atlantic.

We brought our white enamel buckets,
scotched and dented,
down Jockey's lane, past the small field rich in thistles;
the water brimmed in the well, rose pure

over the lightest moss; we turned for home,
the water spilling a long, wandersome trail out of childhood,
the buckets shifting, for their weight,
from one hand to the other. What we miss, at the last,

is the memory of abundance. Now they lie in death, our departed,
and all they have achieved
lies hidden, in that particle of star-being, that fleck of ash
from the great fire, that has been their flesh.

What I will remember, too, are the floppy slippers, his tablets
scattered like old pennies
in the drawer, the stain of a presence on the armchair back.
They placed the ashes of his wicked cat – Calvin – beside him,

clothed his body in the purest alb, to share
the dissolution,
of the body, the catechism, the mathematics.
Now the weight of a phantom bucket

has been drawing my right shoulder down, and my fingers stiffen
from the iron handle; I would be
home again, scuffing shoes against a ditch
where blackberries, after rain, will be glistening like star-dust.

Soul

... heavy as a feather
    from the goldcrest's crown –

swift as the wings
    of the hummingbird – soul

garnering a name for itself –
    and a story, over

seven decades long –
    seeking that root point,

chalice-quiet I
    rarely touch, soul

this one life, with unseen
    unfelt arms upholding

one lucent day on a cliff-face,
    high over dagger-rocks

and a pounding sea –
    soul lemon-bitter,

old-malt-warmed,
    and mother's careful fingers

gathering a tiny body, graced,
    to her yielding breast...

Herbert Lomas (1924–2011)

The whitest and the tiniest, most perfect of feathers
fell from where there could be no feathers, and held

firmly on my sleeve; fly, it whispered, I heard it, only
fly. An afternoon I spent with Bertie, in his upstairs room,

North Gable, Aldeburgh; in the order and disorder
of his library, our speaking touched on angels. I could see –

in the grand mirror above the fireplace – the coldly
exotic North Sea worrying at bulwarks beyond the stones,

unheard persistent music steely as the movement of the stars;
there was dust at the carpet edges, emerald-coloured papering

hung dulled, familial, as if there could be nothing special here,
no nub of poetry, of faith, nothing save the insidious

secretive presence of illness, nothing but fellowship and words,
nothing but the weight of a life most passionately lived, a poet

peregrinus and at home, a citizen of God's – and a lover
of the earthly – city; and our words touched quietly on angels.

in memory

Cadenza

There was something major key about the scythe
with father's big-boned body
slow-waltzing to the rhythm, cadenza, making
meadow-music, no rain expected;

the landrail, in the scurf-grass, had time to crake
and urge her untuned chicks to safety
down into the drain, before windrows, shakings, hayricks
rose in choir and lightly hymned in harvest.

We found surprising the hair-tufts on father's chest,
and mother's levity with the long rake
was a revelation, with the sweet wild honey-nests
discovered in the stubble. We believed, those days,

and there was no question, in Eve and Adam,
the beauty of Ruth in a field, gleaning,
and the Magdalene
turning in the garden towards inexpressible joy.

In the Dark

Dark night and countryside. Cold
descending. Stars
brilliant but sparse, the road damp-sheened, the ditches
treacherous.

I called in earlier, touched
the hardening skin; he – part of it still –
who had moved with contained joy
over his own small fields,

who seeded and harvested,
relished the music of hedgerows, the heart-beat of soil –
was dressed in his best suit, leaving him
looking ill at ease, his swollen fingers

wrapped like tubers
about his beads. The words all spoken, hands shaken,
the procession of cars is slow up the long hill
to the chapel, tail-lights a bright blood-red, and solemn.

Part of it, still.

The bell pealed out across darkness over the lake, where
its own cold creatures turned in their dark,
the stars turning in their ordering, and the vastness
unknowable beyond.

And the grandson, part of it, dressed in his confirmation suit,
well washed and brushed,
glances up at the big
silent woman who holds him firmly by the hand.

The Spoiling Fruit

They dumped the black Ford Prefect
in the drain, down by the hawthorn hedge. In spring

the first white blossoms flourished round it; then
the spread of dogwoods, the bramble push-and-reach

played over it and under, and in a very few years
the old Ford Prefect became root and swell and yield.

Now under the apple trees the reddest apples, wasps
gorging on the spoiling fruit, and sunlight

battening on the whitewashed wall; there gleams
a difficult beauty, the harshest sweetness, and grey

vulgar abundance in the neglected yard; at night
dimly visible clouds play games with the blossoming

stars; vixen feasts beside her cubs, invisible visitors,
at the compost heap. At dawn, at noon, at night

we celebrate what the world has gifted us, the sorrows
of imperfection, the joys of tenderness; our prayers

to the Lord Creator: he is our peace, we are his poem.

PEARL

Pearl

Thomas Merton: *'At the centre point of our being is a point of nothingness which is untouched by sin and illusion, a point of pure truth, a point of spark which belongs entirely to God'*.

Meister Eckhart: *'The eye with which you see God is the eye with which God sees you'*.

I had been listening to Fauré's *Requiem*, a glass
of old-gold whiskey in my hand – seeking

consolation; *in Paradisum deducant te angeli...*
The tenderness of the music

brought the relief of tears, this lullaby of death – its swing-song
ease and loveliness, a presence

sylph-like, silver-dark water flowing down
over a black boulder –

and all my thoughts, as ever, were on Pearl,
all my brooding, dark, angry – near despair.

I

She was sweet, slight, child-lovely, she
was my treasure, Pearl, I would trap her in a nest of gold,
hold her precious, in sheltering arms,
jealous the world might steal her into its stain-and-bustle sorrow; she

was sunshine, laughter :
warmth and nearness at the bed-time story, snow-white, princess
and the pea, the dream;
my snow-bunting, albino blackbird, my polar bear-cub, my lamb.

97

I lost her: she grew silent, pale, those myopic sea-green eyes
grew large in wonder;
she lay motionless in bed, then cot, until I carried her out
in a yew-wood coffin, white

as snowdrop, and laid her down
in the brownest of brown-drab earth, covering her with artificial grass,
and stayed, sorrowing.
I lost her, my Pearl, child-beautiful, snow-white, young and
without spot.

★

It was spring, travelling-time and, high in the humming eucalyptus
cock-robin sang to the glory of his mate.
We were scrubbing the winter scum off our chairs, in the ask of
out-door air,
our portion in the sunlight, our delight;

I have a photo of her, in a dress of amaranth, trimmed
with white; she wears
big, blue-framed glasses, leans forward gazing into the chalice
of a daffodil, part

in childish seriousness
of the earth's loveliness; child-beautiful, vulnerable as snow,
fragile as white crocus, and as strong;
beyond her, early spring-light on rubble-barren clay,

a rusted, tilting gate has opened
on the road, a truck with its yellow cab, its heavy tyres, passes
in world-business; the daffodil
bows its gentle head to Pearl's innocence, my child, beautiful without
spot.

★

There is another photograph:
she is on grass above the shore, a bag of crisps in her left hand,
cornflower-blue dress with black dots
sprinkled, her hair breeze-blown, and all the ocean –

beyond the grass, parked cars, the fleshly bodies – is blue cerulean;
she is stilled to child-sorrow,
sensing perhaps the weight of pain that is to come, the loss,
the foolishness of the wisdom of the world.

I come then, afterwards, every day, to sit
here, by her grave, tending camellia, starflower, anemone,
adding shells, the baby's ear,
beryl, aquamarine, sea-polished glass, like gems, like pearls.

II

Each day
I came, each day
    I wept and tended, knowing
    her flesh and bone now in the roots of earth were a blood
    to the veins of bluebell, tulip, crocus.

Till there came that
Sacred Saturday,
    late spring, warmth in the air.

I sat a while under the maple,
    noon-time, weary;
    at the garden's end the Calvary, the body
    lily-white, the bleeding scarlet and –
    Crucified Christ! I called aloud,

are you living now, my Pearl of wondrous worth, in the light
  of Easter Day?
  Her mound of earth was before me, its
  scant sorrow-scape, her plotted source and destination.

And I was
naked to pain,
  to suffering and sorrow, human, animal and ghost, and groaned
  under the burden.

And stood,
determined, knowing I could
  join her now in death – be my own
  deliverer, the river running fast and deep beyond –

when suddenly, the angelus bell
  called out to me from close at hand and I prayed to Christ
  for my storm-frayed soul, and lay back down, abruptly,
  to save myself, from myself, my wickedness.

Slept, at last,
a troubled, restless sleep.

                             ★

And woke.

The April air
  like an almost visible guardian presence
  shifted slowly through the maple leaves;

I found myself
  disturbed by a silence beyond the stilling of the breeze,
  beyond the cease of birdsong, absence of traffic,
  my own heart thundering,
  blood whispering in its steady stream, here

by her mound of earth, the conch-shells without sea;

stood,
and in the stillness of the moment
  was one with everything:
  the marauding long-tailed tits
  quietened in the tree above me,
  the dragonfly, its diaphanous, its emerald and amethyst
  stained-glass wings, hovering
  over reeds by the river, I was

a demi-semi-quaver in the great symphony and heard
  – out of impossible soundlessness –
  a child-voice call from somewhere near,
  a child-voice something like… but could not be… and I –
  foolish, in the foolish world, feet hurting on the harsh
  pebbles of the path, the ocean sounding from beyond
  and the far-distant high-above drone of the passing of a jet – I

ran, towards the river, that sound, that voice… abandoning
her mound of earth, my sorrow-scape, the sea-shell patterning,
                                    her flowers.

III

Amazed to hear her, grief abandoned me like a plover
leaving shore; to my left I could hear the soft calling
of wood-doves; beyond the graveyard wall

hedgerows were white in a blossoming bridal veil
and the shrubberies red with the blood of fuchsia; all
the gable end of the church stood in a glaze of sunshine,

black-gold bumble-bees and trembling tortoiseshell butterflies
feasted among the blooms; came sharp whingeing notes
of chaffinches, while from amongst the tall, shivering

stems of the snipe-grass came the sharp scolding of the wren.
The river was moving rapidly, its surface smooth and dark; then
from the other side came a girl's laughter; there were stepping-stones,

like lopped-off columns; the water swirled, but I stepped out,
fearlessly; and I walked a while, on water; I thought about
the resurrected Christ, his hand reaching. I did not doubt

a moment, my whole heart singing. I reached shore:

★

and saw her,

IV

woman-child,
    girl-child, child ageless yet a child, there
    on the other shore. She stood, dressed
    in snow-glistening white, as though for first communion,
    as though a bride;

stood
    radiant,
        as if the sunlight shone from her, and she was
        (oh my God!) beautiful,
        and I was stunned and could not cry
        to her; her features flawless, her form
        grace-filled, she smiled towards me,

my
    precious
        girl, still slight, still small, in majesty;

in the whispering of the breeze now,
and in the light itself there was embracing warmth;
trees where she stood were bathed in leaf and blossom,
the chestnut flowers small candelabras of white and pink
while swallow, swift and martin soared and swooped
in the great delight of living.

V

She – my pearl beyond price, lost one, lily-one, mine –

stood before me, lovely, fragrant, innocent, all smiles;
to my knees I fell on the stones, tears falling, my hands reaching
to hold her but I could not, she was there, not-there, flesh, and air;

my knees hurt on the shingles, I was unworthy
before my own beloved; but spoke to her, pleading: 'O my Pearl why
did you leave me? I die without you.' And her voice!

How that voice of music, peace and light, flowed over
into me with such joy and rhapsody I could have stayed,
listening, forever.

★

'Where I am,' she said, 'is heaven and where you are,
I am too; you have not lost me; I am still at home.'
I cried aloud, 'And I, I will not
lose again my pearl beyond price, my lily-one, my own!'

'Wait,' she said, 'patiently, wait, as the maple waits, wait
for the bonds of fleshly suffering to be broken;
wait with all creation
for the glory, wait in hope, till all the twigs and branches

grow into the blessed, the sacred and eternal tree.
There is nothing
to separate you from the love of Christ. Taste and see
the savour of God's creation and every holy creature, world

wounded, healed and resurrected,
for Christ was broken first, and blessed. Listen, for Jesus speaks
person to person, you live already in the kingdom, live
so that you flow into God, child of earth, as I was, as Jesus was,

who died and became part – as you, as I –
of earth, clay of our clay, blood of our blood, and spirit
of our spirit.' Oh then my heart was birdsong, my spirit
in flight like the white flight of the egret.

                                 'And you,' I asked her,

'tell me of you, for I know a father's pain that you died
too young, tell me now your being,
tell me of Jesus, Mary, tell me...'
                           She smiled, and her white and lovely
fingers touched me softly.
                       'My being,' she said, 'is Hallelujah,

and all my fire Hosanna.

We
  innumerable
    multitudes of the blessed,' she said, 'we move
    across the scaffoldings of creation, labouring, in joy,
    in the bathing love of the Creator. Guardian spirits
    of tree and star and galaxy, the great and joyful task
    of drawing the evolving universe to fulfilment
    in the presence and blessing of the holiest and best.'

                              ★

She paused: 'Be a light to the world,' she said, 'the night
is far gone, it is time to rise from sleep, put on
the Lord Jesus, dress yourself in light.' Her hand touched me:

'Rise', she said, 'don't, Dad, be on your knees before me.'
I looked up, touched
by the name, and her unsurpassable beauty swept
my breath away. Stood, stiff, a little sore,
but my whole being sang for joy. I gazed at her, my

Pearl, whom
   I cherished, whom
      I cherish still. Her eyes a bright sea-green, on her breast
      a pearl, periwinkle blue.

She moved
   a little
      towards the river; her feet scarce touched
      the ground, I plodded after, my heart
      pounding. As we walked she spoke:

'It is the great
   unfolding drama, the beautiful excess of universe,
   anemone and allium, the wren, toucan, the albatross,
   eucalyptus, acanthus, the redwood forests,
   the grain of sand, the water-drop, the billion-oceaned-galaxy...'

and I
   in bitterness still:
      'the greed of banker, builder, senator,
      swollen belly of the famished child,
      Goliath warriors pounding down the children of the poor...'

She smiled,
   there was no sadness in the smile; and said –
      'anvil of hammer in the inner ear, fingernails of the newborn babe,
      Titian, Homer, Heloïse and Abelard, Pushkin, Rodin, Brahms...
      Without black, no white,
      without time, no growth, without root no blossom,
      without death, no life and Jesus crucified
      denies to the human soul its refusal still to love...'

★

We had reached the river's edge where darkling waters harried past;
                       she stepped
out onto chaos, I cried aloud in fear, but she turned
and took my hand and I walked, too, on the churning waters, and we –
like old-time lovers – strode on clouds and water-drops, and reached
the other bank where the yellow iris grew and the high reeds,
the golden harvest of the meadows and the silver seedlings of the sky.

She led me to the maple tree, by the cemetery wall;

'I am gardener, too, of the earth,' she said, 'tender
of its loveliness; carer of the wild and ordered forests of the galaxies,
of the flower-beds of souls planted in the love of the Holiest. Be

open,' she said, 'to surprise, to the sacred earth and the body and soul
of the emergent universe...'
               her voice fading slowly, and her form,
and I reached for her, my whole body feeble now, but my spirit
firm, kin at last to pearl and the labours of ocean, to Pearl
and the works of love... heavy my eyes, my darling
merging back into the light of day, to the gossamer
dusting of the air...

★

and awoke – and it was autumn: late
in my living, the scarlet veins
of the fallen maple leaves about me,

the wind making loud death-rattle amongst the branches;
I would start again, leaf-combing, lane-keeping, husbanding;
I stood; there was one cock-robin high in the bared-back tree

singing brightly; there was something cold in my closed fist;
I opened it: on my palm a large pearl, rounded as hailstone,
perfect as snow, glistening; I held it out, sunlight

sparkled on its surface and I fancied
it was growing moist, starting
to melt; at its heart a tiny pulsing, as if it lived;

it was softening, yielding; I raised it to my mouth
where it melted slowly on my tongue, its purity, its living,
and I was fed by it, and my thirst was quenched.

Acknowledgements

Warwick Review, Agenda, Ambit, PN Review, Poem (ed. Fiona Sampson), *Rialto, London Magazine, Poetry Review* (UK), *The Tablet* (UK); *Christian Century* (Chicago), *Atlanta Review* (ed. Brian Turner), *Beloit Poetry Journal, Consequence Magazine, Stony Thursday Book* (ed. Paddy Bushe), *Stony Thursday Book* (ed. Peter Sirr), *Irish Times, Lighter Craft – Poems for Peter Denman, SHOp, Crannóg, Indian Poetry Journal, Irish Pages* (ed. Chris Agee),*Berryman's Fate* (ed. Philip Coleman), *The Stinging Fly*.

The sequence 'According to Lydia' was first published in *Performing the Word: a Festschrift for Ronan Drury* (ed. Enda McDonagh, Columba Press 2014); 'The Upright Piano' appeared in the anthology *Fermata* edited by Eva Bourke and Vincent Woods.